PHILIPS

PHILIPS

Philips Medical Systems

with our compliments   **RSNA 1990**

Seasons

A Book for Special Days from The Art Institute of Chicago

Cover and endpaper illustration:

Georges Seurat (French, 1859–1891)
Sunday Afternoon on the Island of La Grande Jatte (details), 1884–86
Oil on canvas, 207.6 × 308 cm.
Helen Birch Bartlett Memorial
Collection, 1926.224

All reproductions are details of works
in the collections of The Art Institute
of Chicago.

Coordinator: Linda J. Cohn

Text by Jeanne Sellnau Osgood

Editor: Elizabeth A. Pratt

Designer: Ann W. Gross

ISBN 0-87654-061-2

Printed and bound in Singapore

Published by Pomegranate Calendars & Books
Box 808022, Petaluma, CA 94975

Seasons

The rhythm of the seasons, whether pronounced or subtle, is a universal experience shared by all cultures through the ages. The change of the seasons during the year paradoxically provides a sense of both variety and predictability, of both the passing of time and the renewal of life. Artists have represented the seasons in ways that reveal the multiplicity of experiences of this familiar phenomenon, each interpretation enriching our view of this ordinary yet almost magical cyclical drama.

The permanent collections of The Art Institute of Chicago include many representations of the seasons, most of which depict the land itself. This seemingly obvious vehicle is in fact the most modern one. Before landscape was considered a major, independent theme in art, the seasons were personified—shown as figures involved in the "labors of the months" or activities of a particular part of the year. Classical Roman sarcophagi, for example, were sometimes decorated with figures identified as the Four Seasons: each carried a characteristic attribute, such as a slaughtered animal for fall and winter or a basket of flowers or grapes for spring or summer. In the Middle Ages, this convention was expanded to show the labors of individual months in the context of God's larger order unifying earthly and heavenly existence with seasonal and eternal time. In the sculptures found on the façades of the great cathedrals at Autun, Chartres, Amiens, and Notre-Dame in Paris, depictions of work and seasonal time are combined with sacred images to form the larger system of cosmological time and everlasting life. The tilling of the soil, the task God gave Adam, is the most often exploited theme, along with its variations of harvesting, threshing grain, and pressing grapes.

The role of the personified seasons continued into the 18th century with such well-known examples as Jean Antoine Watteau's (French, 1684–1721) *Seasons* (c. 1715–16), in which the products of the land—wheat and grapes—are the accouterments of summer and autumn. In this work, an old man winter huddles near a fire and blows cold winds; and the flower-goddess spring frolics with a gentle young Zephyr. This second image links the themes of springtime, love, and youth, a combination that gave rise to countless paintings of love scenes set in verdant pastoral surroundings. Another 18th-century painter, François Boucher, is perhaps best known for such idyllic scenes.

Man's view of his interactions with nature was expressed in the 17th century in the form of inhabited landscapes, popular especially in the Netherlands and France. While the paintings by Hobbema and Claude Lorrain illustrated in this book represent different artistic inclinations—the former a more realistic, mundane view of country life and the latter an idealized, imaginary depiction of a pagan procession—both landscapes are characterized by the sense of tranquility, harmony, and order man felt in nature. Such an attitude gave way in the 19th century, however, to the exploration of the expressive potential of landscape. Romantic painters such as J.M.W. Turner, although influenced deeply by Claude and by the Dutch painters, interpreted nature and man's relation to it in a more dramatic and often apocalyptic manner. Turner's painting *Valley of Aosta — Snowstorm, Avalanche, and Thunderstorm* is an utterly malevolent winter scene, with the huddling figures in the lower right seemingly doomed to end in its fury. This chaotic outburst of energy in which natural forces are raised to the level of cosmic cataclysm is far removed from the peaceful nature of Claude's works.

With the advent of Impressionism, artists such as Claude Monet, Vincent van Gogh, and Pierre Auguste Renoir returned to a more gentle vision of the landscape to show us its everlasting yet everchanging expressions throughout the year. Monet's haystacks series almost epitomizes the Impressionists' fascination with chronicling the effects of the seasons. Monet actually studied the haystacks throughout the entire year, recording his experiences in narrative fashion as colors that cloak the stacks, changing from picture to picture, from season to season. In the 19th century, too, we see a return to the association between the seasons and labor: cornhusking in Eastman Johnson's painting; gathering and chopping wood in works by Alexander Wyant and Currier and Ives; and clearing fields in Camille Pissarro's *Haying Time*. The artists of the 19th and 20th centuries also celebrated the leisures of the seasons. Industrialization provided free time for the middle class and, whether in the cities or countryside, people participating in the pastimes of each season—strolling, reading, playing croquet, boating, fishing, and ice skating—became popular subjects. Finally, other turn-of-the-century artists such as Puvis de Chavannes and Henri Rousseau turned back to the 17th century and the tradition of idealized, imaginary settings in which the fertility of the land suggests the creativity of man.

This evolving vision of man's interaction with nature is perhaps most beautifully revealed by Japanese artists, for whom change throughout the year and growth throughout a lifetime were often symbolically interrelated. Sei Shonagon, a 10th-century authoress, suggested this relationship when she wrote of "Things that Do Not Linger for a Moment" in her *Pillow Book*, a collection of amusing thoughts and reflections:

A boat with hoisted sails.

People's ages.

The Four Seasons.

Gnarled old trees, for example, like those in two screens by Tosa Mitsuoki were regarded as symbols of fortitude and rejuvenation.

These seemingly eternal trees explode each spring with blossoms that are continually transformed throughout the summer until they achieve their warm orange fall color.

The modern views of the seasons that make up the bulk of this book have been enriched by the accumulation of and borrowing from past traditions. Whether personifications or simpler depictions of the landscape itself, inhabited or not, the images here serve to remind us, like the trees in Mitsuoki's screens, of the cycle in which we all take part and of the reappearance of the past in the present, again and again.

SAKAI, HOITSU (Japanese, 1761–1828)
Mandarin Ducks in Snow
Colors and gold on paper, 160 × 166.5 cm.
Gift of Robert Allerton, 1957.244

Hōitsu, a poet, Buddhist monk, and painter, combined lyricism and realism in this screen. The austere design compels us to recognize winter's essence in the fragile, icy branches and huddled ducks; yet the flowers emerging through the snow express the hope of spring.

January

1

2

3

4

5

6

7

CAMILLE PISSARRO (French, 1830–1903)
Rabbit Warren at Pontoise, Snow, 1879
Oil on canvas, 59.2 × 72.3 cm.
Gift of Marshall Field, 1964.200

The brutal winter of 1879 in France obscured
the land with deep snow. Pissarro's depiction of the stark landscape of Pontoise
conveys the sense of helplessness against
nature the inhabitants must have felt.

January

8

9

10

11

12

13

14

GEORGE BELLOWS (American, 1882–1925)
Love of Winter, 1914
Oil on canvas, 81.6 × 101.7 cm.
Friends of American Art Collection, 1914.1018

At the turn of the century, many American painters turned to the American scene and sought to capture the look of life in our land. Bellows, a sports enthusiast, painted this colorful view of skaters enjoying the winter with directness and spontaneity.

January

15

16

17

18

19

20

21

CLAUDE MONET (French, 1840–1926)
Haystack, Winter, Giverny, 1891
Oil on canvas, 66 × 93 cm.
Mr. and Mrs. Martin A. Ryerson Collection,
1933.1155

Monet's desire to record the nuances wrought
by time on the fields around Giverny resulted in at least thirty paintings of grain-
stacks. Each provides a distinctive expression
of the fleeting nature of light and the
seasons.

January

22

23

24

25

26

27

28

CURRIER AND IVES (American firm, active 1835–1907)
A Snowy Morning, 1864
Colored lithograph, 28.1 × 40.8 cm.
Gift of the Print and Drawing Club, 1928.666

The lithographs of Nathaniel Currier and J. Merritt Ives have been popular in America since the mid-19th century due to their accessibility and anecdotal, familiar nature. This image combines the tasks of winter with its pleasures in a landscape of new-fallen snow.

Jan./Feb.

29

30

31

1

2

3

4

JOHN HENRY TWACHTMAN (American, 1853–1902)
Icebound, c. 1889
Oil on canvas, 64.1 × 76.5 cm.
Friends of American Art Collection, 1917.200

Twachtman painted the Hemlock Pool on his farm in Connecticut through different seasons just as Monet did his haystacks. The undulating pattern of blue and white in *Icebound* suggests the fluidity of melting snow.

February

5

6

7

8

9

10

11

VINCENT VAN GOGH (Dutch, 1853–1890)
Montmartre, probably c. 1886
Oil on canvas, 43.6 × 33 cm.
Helen Birch Bartlett Memorial Collection,
1926.202

Van Gogh arrived in Paris for the second
time in 1886, when his painting underwent
an abrupt change under the strong influ-
ences of Impressionism and Japanese wood-
cuts (see Hiroshige, Dec. 24–31). In this
scene of a cold winter day on Montmartre,
the strong vertical and diagonal elements
tell of the Japanese influence.

February

12 _____

13 _____

14 _____

15 _____

16 _____

17 _____

18 _____

JOSEPH MALLORD WILLIAM TURNER
(British, 1775–1851)
Valley of Aosta—Snowstorm, Avalanche and Thunderstorm, 1836/37
Oil on canvas, 92.2 × 123 cm.
Frederick T. Haskell Collection, 1947.513

Turner visited the Valley of Aosta in the summer of 1836 and could therefore only imagine the violent fury of the Alpine winter. But man's powerlessness in the face of nature's changes and energy is keenly felt in this painting.

February

19

20

21

22

23

24

25

CAMILLE PISSARRO (French, 1830–1903)
The Banks of the Marne in Winter, 1866
Oil on canvas, 91.8 × 150.2 cm.
Mr. and Mrs. Lewis Larned Coburn Memorial Fund, 1957.306

Although this is not a snow scene, the presence of winter is felt in the bleak emptiness of the land and in the cold, threatening sky. Pissarro's bold use of open space is intensified by the isolated elements of the picture—the small figures, thin trees, and buildings.

Feb./Mar.

26

27

28   29

1

2

3

4

C. Pissarro 1871

CAMILLE PISSARRO (French, 1830–1903)
The Crystal Palace, 1871
Oil on canvas, 47.2 × 73.5 cm.
Gift of Mr. and Mrs. B.E. Bensinger,
1972.1164

Pissarro, in London in 1871 to escape France's
volatile political climate, has captured the
chilly atmosphere of an early spring day in
the city. Both the foliage of the urban landscape and the Crystal Palace at the left
seem to symbolize the promise of changes
yet to come—summer and man's predom-
inence over natural forces.

March

5

6

7

8

9

10

11

GUSTAVE CAILLEBOTTE (French, 1848–1894)
Paris, A Rainy Day (Intersection of the Rue de Turin and Rue de Moscou), 1877
Oil on canvas, 212.2 × 276.2 cm.
Charles H. and Mary F. S. Worcester Fund, 1964.336

Although the landscape of Caillebotte's Paris is absolutely manmade, nature still dominates in the form of a spring shower. The clear, logical order of the city is softened by the rain and mist; weather challenges the stability of the picture with it's ephemeral nature.

March

12

13

14

15

16

17

18

CLAUDE GELLEE (called Le Lorrain)
(French, 1600–1682)
Landscape with Sacrificial Procession, 1673
Oil on canvas, 101.7 × 127.3 cm.
Robert A. Waller Memorial Fund, 1941.1020

For Claude, the painted landscape was one
of perfection, solemnity, and grandeur,
intended to provoke profound emotion as
well as inspiring thoughts. This example
reveals Claude's extraordinary view of harmony between man and nature.

March

19

20

21

22

23

24

25

TOSA, MITSUOKI (Japanese, 1617–1691)
Cherry Blossoms (Spring)
Colors on silk, 130.5 × 272 cm.
Kate S. Buckingham Collection, 1977.156

This screen and its autumnal mate (see Oct. 15–21) were an imperial commission, painted for the Empress Tofuku Mon-in. Though they served a primarily functional purpose, the screens also served to carry expressions of the land and the seasons indoors.

Mar./Apr.

26

27

28

29

30

31

1

MAURICE PRENDERGAST (American,
1861–1924)
The Mall, Central Park, 1901
Watercolor, 38.8 × 56.7 cm.
Olivia Shaler Swan Collection, 1939.341

Groups of people in public places fascinated
Prendergast. In this park scene, the figures
have become brightly colored, balloonlike
shapes that seem to float, wafted about by
the springtime breeze.

April

2

3

4

5

6

7

8

VINCENT VAN GOGH (Dutch, 1853–1890)
Fishing in Spring
Oil on canvas, 50.5 × 60 cm.
Gift of Charles Deering McCormick, Brooks
McCormick, and Roger McCormick, 1965.1169

Adopting the rich palette, atmospheric
concerns, and even the leisure-time subject
matter of the Impressionists, van Gogh's
picture celebrates the pleasures of spring.
Although the subject suggests quiet tranquility, the angular brushwork and intense
colors betray the artist's, and perhaps
nature's, restless energy.

April

9

10

11

12

13

14

15

JOHN SINGER SARGENT (American, 1856–1925)
Woodsheds, Tyrol, c. 1914
Watercolor, 40.8 × 53.5 cm.
Olivia Shaler Swan Memorial Collection, 1933.506

Before the advent of World War I, Sargent passed the warm months in the Alps, recording the look of the rural world with his usual facile brushwork. These farmyard sheds must have appealed to Sargent's love of color, contrast, and the play of light and shadow.

April

16

17

18

19

20

21

22

PIERRE CECILE PUVIS DE CHAVANNES
(French, 1824–1898)
The Sacred Grove, c. 1884
Oil on canvas, 93 × 231 cm.
Potter Palmer Collection, 1922.445

This painting is a copy of the artist's large
mural in the Palais des Arts in Lyon, France.
Assembled in a tranquil springtime landscape, the three Arts and nine Muses evoke
a mood of enlightenment and timelessness.

April

23

24

25

26

27

28

29

WILLIAM MERRITT CHASE (American, 1849–1916)
The Park, c. 1888
Oil on canvas, 34.6 × 49.9 cm.
Bequest of Dr. John Jay Ireland, 1968.88

Chase was particularly drawn to the public parks populated by city-dwellers in New York City and Brooklyn in the 1880's. *The Park* is delicately colored but strong in composition, the result being a careful balance of figures and space.

Apr./May

30

1

2

3

4

5

6

PIERRE AUGUSTE RENOIR (French, 1841–1919)
On the Terrace, 1881
Oil on canvas, 100.5 × 81 cm.
Mr. and Mrs. Lewis Larned Coburn Memorial Collection, 1933.455

Springtime must have been Renoir's favorite season. The dull, tedious winter could hardly have inspired the man who called snow "that leprosy of nature." Only in spring did the land actually return to match his arcadian vision of pleasure and warmth.

May

7

8

9

10

11

12

13

FRANCOIS BOUCHER (French, 1703–1770)
Pense-t-il aux Raisins? (Is he thinking about
the Grapes?), 1747
Oil on canvas, 80.8 × 68.5 cm.
Purchased from Martha E. Leverone Bequest, 1973.304

The ironic title of this painting has an obvious answer. All details evoke sensuality, love, and fertility—all of which have come to be associated with spring.

May

14

15

16

17

18

19

20

THEODORE H. ROBINSON (American, 1852–1896)
The Valley of Arconville, 1887/1889
Oil on canvas, 45.7 × 55.5 cm.
Friends of American Art Collection, 1941.11

Robinson, an American working near Giverny, Monet's home, chose a hillside view for his reading figure. We can easily appreciate her sense of retreat from daily life in the village below as she basks in the warmth of a sunny spring day.

May

21

22

23

24

25

26

27

FRANCESCO PAOLO MICHETTI (Italian,
1851–1929)
Springtime and Love, 1878
Oil on canvas, 94.6 × 184.3 cm.
A.A. Munger Collection, 1901.429

Michetti's painting is an uninhibited vision
of springtime perfection in the tradition of
a bacchanal. This is a time of youthful in-
nocence, energy, and repose as the pink-
skinned children prance, play, and lounge
under the brilliant sky.

May/June

28

29

30

31

1

2

3

MARY CASSATT (American, 1844–1926)
Woman Reading in A Garden, 1880
Oil on canvas, 90.2 × 72.7 cm.
Gift of Mrs. Albert J. Beveridge in memory
of her aunt, Delia Spencer Field, 1938.18

The solitude of reading is made explicit in
this portrait of the artist's sister. Lydia seems
oblivious to the beauty around her; at the
same time her concentration contributes to
the sense of peacefulness that characterizes
the work.

June

4

5

6

7

8

9

10

ANONYMOUS (American)
Mountain Village, c. 1880–1915
Oil on canvas, 46.1 × 64.9 cm.
Gift of Edgar William and Bernice Chrysler
Garbisch, 1980.736

With simplicity and directness, the artist of
this landscape shares with us the joys of
summer in a small mountain village. The
crisply detailed boats are arranged sym-
metrically, echoing the harmony and order
of the landscape itself.

June

11

12

13

14

15

16

17

JOHN SINGER SARGENT (American, 1856–1925)
The Fountain, Villa Torlonia, Frascati, 1907
Oil on canvas, 71.4 × 56.5 cm.
Friends of American Art Collection, 1914.57

Sargent spent the summers of 1906 and 1907 in Italy and the Alps, painting numerous images of verdant gardens and luxurious villas. Here he captures one of summer's—and his own—pleasures in this portrait of his friends and students Wilfred and Jane de Glehn.

June

18

19

20

21

22

23

24

VINCENT VAN GOGH (Dutch, 1853–1890)
The Garden of the Poets, 1888
Oil on canvas, 73 × 92.1 cm.
Mr. and Mrs. Lewis Larned Coburn Memorial Collection, 1933.433

The strong sun of southern France was thrilling to van Gogh, for in it he saw simplified form and purified color. This aggressively painted canvas was his gift to Gauguin whom he welcomed to Arles as "the new local poet."

June/July

25

26

27

28

29

30

1

SUSAN MERRITT (American, active 1850's)
Fourth of July Picnic at Weymouth Landing,
Massachusetts, c. 1853
Watercolor and collage, 66 × 91.5 cm.
Bequest of Elizabeth Vaughan, 1950.1846

The gathering of this community to cele-
brate America's independence is appro-
priately set in a welcoming, lush summer
landscape. Merritt's style is direct and legi-
ble and her subject suggests the relationship
between man and the land.

July

2

3

4

5

6

7

8

ALFRED SISLEY (French, 1839–1899)
Watering Place at Marly, 1875
Oil on canvas, 39.5 × 56.2 cm.
Gift of Mrs. Clive Runnells, 1971.875

The ruins of the Château de Marly, once an
elegant aristocratic retreat, were popular
summertime strolling grounds in the 19th
century. With Sisley's attention to the
changing pattern of clouds and sun, and
the resulting shadows, the old site acquires
a sense of transience, emphasized by the
ruined state of man's constructions.

July

9

10

11

12

13

14

15

HENRI ROUSSEAU (Le Douanier) (French,
1844–1910)
The Waterfall, 1910
Oil on canvas, 116.2 × 150.2 cm.
Helen Birch Bartlett Memorial Collection,
1926.262

Rousseau's tropical dreams were born from
his vigorous imagination. He had no need
to travel further than the Jardin des Plantes
in Paris, which inspired this imaginary
world, an equatorial utopia of mysterious
and energetic harmonies.

July

16

17

18

19

20

21

22

CHILDE HASSAM (American, 1859–1935)
New England Headlands, 1899
Oil on canvas, 68.9 × 68.9 cm.
Walter H. Schulze Memorial Collection,
1930.349

In 1899, Hassam lived in Gloucester and
painted panoramic views of life along the
New England coast. This one is outstanding
for the balance between the clear geometry
of the nearby houses and the hill and the
scintillating summer airiness of the distance.

23

24

25

26

27

28

29

GEORGES SEURAT (French, 1859–1891)
Sunday Afternoon on the Island of La Grande Jatte, 1884–86
Oil on canvas, 207.6 × 308 cm.
Helen Birch Bartlett Memorial Collection, 1926.224

Everyday life is transformed into a summertime pagaent in arcadia on the Grande Jatte. Although Seurat was intrigued by the challenge of representing contemporary life, he also sought to eternalize it by imposing order on the environment.

July/Aug.

30

31

1

2

3

4

5

MEINDERT HOBBEMA (Dutch, 1638–1709)
The Watermill with the Great Red Roof, c. 1670
Oil on canvas, 81.3 × 110 cm.
Gift of Mr. and Mrs. Frank G. Logan,
1894.1031

With pride in their national prosperity,
17th-century Dutch painters typically turned
to the local landscapes as a symbolic subject. This lush summer scene reveals nature's gifts to man—the vegetation, the
energy of water, and the sustenance of light.

August

6

7

8

9

10

11

12

HENRI CROSS (French, 1856–1910)
Beach at Cabasson, 1891/92
Oil on canvas, 65.3 × 92.3 cm.
Bette and Neison Harris, Charles H. and
Mary F. S. Worcester Collection, and L.L.
and A.S. Coburn funds, Kate L. Brewster
Collection, 1983.513

Cross lived in Cabasson on the Côte d'Azur,
an isolated retreat whose setting was en-
ariched by the sea, sun, and nearby mountains. With utter meticulousness, he captured the tranquility of a hot summer day.

August

13

14

15

16

17

18

19

PIERRE AUGUSTE RENOIR (French, 1841–1919)
Near the Lake, c. 1880
Oil on canvas, 47.5 × 56.3 cm.
Potter Palmer Collection, 1922.439

This view consists of everything that was summer to Renoir: fair-weather pleasure seekers are embraced by the sun-dappled landscape. Such agreeable, relaxing images were his antidote to the rapidity of social and industrial change in the late 19th century.

August

20

21

22

23

24

25

26

CLAUDE MONET (French, 1840–1926)
On the Seine at Bennecourt, 1868
Oil on canvas, 81.5 × 100.7 cm.
Potter Palmer Collection, 1922.427

Our view of the Seine is shared here with
Camille Doncieux, who was to become the
artist's wife. Her gaze directs us from the
coolness of the shaded foreground in which
she sits, across the slow-moving river, to
the houses and cliffs brightly lit by the
summer sun.

Aug./Sept.

27

28

29

30

31

1

2

WINSLOW HOMER (American, 1836–1910)
Croquet Scene, 1866
Oil on canvas, 40.6 × 66.0 cm.
Friends of American Art Collection, 1942.35

Croquet was becoming a popular summertime sport for men and women in America
when Homer painted this picture. The
breezy season is made palpable in the lifted
hat ribbons and swaying dresses, all sharply
outlined by the glare of the sun.

September

3

4

5

6

7

8

9

THOMAS WORTHINGTON WHITTREDGE
(American, 1820–1910)
Forest Interior, 1882
Oil on canvas, 69.8 × 69.8 cm.
Roger McCormick Fund, 1981.643

In contrast to the spectacular, open pan-
orama by Cole (see Nov. 19–25), Whittredge's
Forest Interior is intimate, enclosed, and
soothing. Sunlight penetrates the dense
stream-fed growth and leads our view to
the center of the forest.

September

10

11

12

13

14

15

16

GEORGE INNESS (American, 1825–1894)
Home of the Heron, 1893
Oil on canvas, 76.2 × 117.9 cm.
Edward B. Butler Collection, 1911.31

For Inness, art was "nothing but tempera-
ment, an expression of your feelings." *Home
of the Heron* evokes a mood of mystery, as
well as a somber harmony, through the
elimination of detail by the dense atmosphere and deep color.

September

17

18

19

20

21

22

23

WILLIAM SIDNEY MOUNT (American, 1807–1868)
The Residence of the Late Thomas Mills, Esq., Mills Pond, Long Island, 1847
Oil on panel, 26.1 × 34.3 cm.
Marian and Samuel Klasstorner and Ada Turnbull Hertle funds, 1981.10

Mount is less well-known for freely executed paintings in the out-of-doors, such as this painting, than for his records of daily life. The subject was a neighbor's house near his home at Stony Brook, Long Island.

September

24

25

26

27

28

29

30

CAMILLE PISSARRO (French, 1830–1903)
Haying Time, 1892
Oil on canvas, 65.5 × 81.3 cm.
Gift of Bruce Borland, 1961.791

France's agricultural heritage was repeatedly celebrated by Pissarro. This fall field, punctuated by the remnants of an orchard and the sturdy, hard-working peasants, is a symbol of the nation's rural wealth and the dignity of labor.

October

1

2

3

4

5

6

7

EUGENE BOUDIN (French, 1824–1898)
Approaching Storm, 1864
Oil on panel, 36.6 × 57.9 cm.
Mr. and Mrs. Lewis Larned Coburn Memorial Collection, 1938.1276

Boudin's practice of open-air painting, which he shared with the young Monet, resulted in the vivid spontaneity of this picture. The Norman beach with its chic bourgeois gathering is the setting for this study of the changeable weather. Even the rolling changing houses attest to the impermanence of the season.

October

8

9

10

11

12

13

14

TOSA, MITSUOKI (Japanese, 1617–1691)
Maple Leaves (Autumn)
Colors on silk, 130.5 × 272 cm.
Kate S. Buckingham Collection, 1977.157

Mitsuoki, a favorite of the imperial court,
painted this screen and its mate, *Cherry
Blossoms*, for the Emperor Dowager (see
Mar. 26–Apr. 1). The sun-dried maple leaves
reflect the transience of the season, while
the sturdy, lichen-covered trunk suggests
the tree's endurance through time.

October

15

16

17

18

19

20

21

SANFORD ROBINSON GIFFORD (American, 1823–1880)
Kauterskill Clove, Catskill Mountains, 1880
Oil on canvas, 33.8 × 27.3 cm.
Goodman and Wirt D. Walker funds, 1982.270

This luminous painting is a superb example of Gifford's attempts to paint the effects of light on land and water. Here, the dissolving forms and heavy atmosphere recall an early fall morning in the Adirondacks.

October

22

23

24

25

26

27

28

WINSLOW HOMER (American, 1836–1910)
For to be A Farmer's Boy (Old English Song), 1887
Watercolor over pencil, 35.8 × 51 cm.
Anonymous gift in memory of Edward Carson Waller, 1963.760

Life close to the land is monumentalized by this sturdy lad. Homer combined colorful pattern, still atmosphere, and exuberant brushwork in this tribute to human labor and the bounty of the land.

Oct./Nov.

29

30

31

1

2

3

4

ALEXANDER HELWIG WYANT (American, 1836–1892)
Autumn in New Hampshire, 1874/75
Oil on canvas, 46.0 × 76.2 cm.
Cyrus Hall McCormick Fund, 1947.26

The mutability of the land is exposed in this crystalline view of New England. Wyant has not only recorded nature's seasonal effects but also those of man, as the forests are cleared and the land is cultivated.

November

5

6

7

8

9

10

11

CLAUDE MONET (French, 1840–1926)
Two Haystacks, 1891
Oil on canvas, 64.8 × 99.8 cm.
Mr. and Mrs. Lewis Larned Coburn Memorial Collection, 1933.444

Monet's haystacks (see also Jan. 22–28) embody many aspects of the tradition of representing the seasons. Human labor is condensed in the products of the field and contemplation is inspired by the apparent paradox of fleeting light and constant seasonal change.

November

12

13

14

15

16

17

18

THOMAS COLE (American, 1801–1848)
Niagara Falls, 1830
Oil on panel, 47.9 × 60.7 cm.
Friends of American Art Collection, 1946.396

The pagaent of nature was exploited by
American landscapists in the early 19th
century. In Cole's example, two Indians
witness the eternal power of the falls and
the surrounding transformations of the
seasons.

November

19

20

21

22

23

24

25

EASTMAN JOHNSON (American, 1824–1906)
Husking Bee, Island of Nantucket, 1876
Oil on canvas, 69.2 × 137.6 cm.
Potter Palmer Collection, 1922.444

The ritual of husking corn in November for winter storage is celebrated here in Johnson's recording of a distinctively American genre scene. The freely executed brushwork of his style suggests the influence of the late 19th-century school of painting originating in Munich.

26

27

28

29

30

1

2

JOHN LA FARGE (American, 1835–1910)
Snow Field, Morning, 1864
Oil on panel, 30.5 × 25.1 cm.
Restricted gift of Mrs. Frank L. Sulzberger
in memory of Frank L. Sulzberger, 1981.287

La Farge has with a minimum of elements
captured the mood of a bleak mid-winter
day in Roxbury, Massachusetts. The painting reveals the artist's familiarity with contemporary French theories that would become the foundation of Impressionism.

December

3

4

5

6

7

8

9

CHILDE HASSAM (American, 1859–1935)
Winter Landscape with Figures, 1902
Oil on canvas, 61.5 × 51.4 cm.
Gift from the Estate of Edna H. Loewenstein,
1980.289

Returning to New York City from Europe in
1889, Hassam proceeded to take an Im-
pressionist approach to the American scene.
In this view, probably Fifth Avenue at Central Park, Hassam's thick, broad brushwork
effectively conveys the snow covering the
city.

December

10

11

12

13

14

15

16

GEORGE HUNT (English, 19th century)
Approach to Christmas (after J. Pollard)
Etching, hand colored, 38.5 × 52 cm.
Gift of Mrs. Charles Netcher in memory of
Charles Netcher II, 1925.294

Just as the prints of Currier and Ives help
preserve 19th-century America (see Jan.
29–Feb. 4), images such as Hunt's and
Pollard's are visual records of life in 19th-
century London. This precisely detailed
aquatint is filled with colorful incidents that
convey the season's excitement.

December

17

18

19

20

21

22

23

ICHIRYUSAI, HIROSHIGE (Japanese, 1797–1858)
Snow Scene (Fan Print), 1852
Woodblock print, 23.2 × 28.4 cm.
Clarence Buckingham Collection of Japanese Prints, 1943.692

Hiroshige here depicts the mood of the season with ice-covered branches, gently falling snow, and even foot prints in the snow—details that are exemplary of the Japanese reverence and sensitivity to nature.

December

24

25

26

27

28

29

30   31